>>> SKITS FOR STUDENT MINISTRY

12 SKETCHES

RETELL
BIBLE NARRATIVES
FROM ANOTHER ANGLE

12 SKETCHES

Standard
PUBLISHING
Bringing the Word to Life™

Cincinnati, Ohio

Published by Standard Publishing, Cincinnati, Ohio

www.standardpub.com

Copyright © 2008 Standard Publishing

Printed in: USA

Project editor: Kelly Carr

Cover and interior design: The DesignWorks Group

ISBN 978-0-7847-2251-0

14 13 12 11 10 09 08   9 8 7 6 5 4 3 2 1

CONTENTS

We're glad you picked up this book. The sketches take narratives from the Bible and retell those historical situations from unique, current perspectives. There are parodies of popular culture as well as biblical people put in contemporary situations to draw students into the action.

Stories resonate with students. By constructing modern-day stories from accounts in the Bible, the ideas will capture teens' attention and stick in their minds. Those acting out the skits as well as those watching will realize that God's Word truly IS relevant to their daily lives!

We all know students who have a dramatic flair for life, and that's who we had in mind when we created these skits. Each skit is created for teens to use their skills in dramatizing biblical narratives. These skits are limited—in a good way: limited to a few cast members, a few lines to learn, and a few props.

So whether you are giving a youth group talk, sharing at a retreat session, teaching a Sunday school lesson, or preaching a sermon, the skits in this book will get your teens in on the act!

Use this skit to retell the biblical narrative of Achan and discuss
the consequences of our sin.

Joshua 6 and 7

three signs labeled: "Sheep," "Cow," "Chicken"
tape to stick the three signs on the actors or string to hang the
signs around the actors' necks
a bunch of paper wads
(optional) other items for actors to wear to indicate the type of
animals they are (ex: cotton balls for Sheep, bell for Cow,
feathers for Chicken)

Sheep—can be male or female
Cow—female
Chicken—male

OFFSTAGE HELPERS (at least two)—will throw paper wads onto stage at the actors throughout skit and will appear onstage briefly at end of skit

Actors should be on stage and have the signs saying "Sheep," "Cow," or "Chicken" attached to their chests or hanging around their necks. Actors may do as much or as little sound effects or animated movements as they'd like to represent the animals. OFFSTAGE HELPERS (need at least one person on either side of the stage) will begin the scene by throwing several paper wads out onto the stage at the animals. They should throw sometimes at or sometimes near the three actors. They should keep throwing paper wads occasionally, especially at places indicated in the script but also give breaks for the actors to say their lines.

SHEEP: *[extended vowel words should sound similar to the* baa *of a sheep]* Whaaaaaaaaaat are we doing here again? Whyyyyyy are those people throwing rocks at us?

[OFFSTAGE HELPERS throw directly at SHEEP, and SHEEP dodges.]

COW: You can blame that on our owner, Achan.

CHICKEN: What's his problem? And why are he and his family standing over there in the valley and dodging rocks like us?

COW: Achan stole something.

SHEEP: Whaaat's that got to do with us?

COW: I'll tell you what I heard last night. Just watch my back. I don't need a rock in my head.

[OFFSTAGE HELPERS throw and hit COW—aim for her head.]

COW: *[grabs head or whatever part of body gets hit by paper wad]* Ow! I'm hit! I'm hit!

CHICKEN: *[whispers to SHEEP]* Maybe it'll knock some sense into her.

COW: I heard that. You *are* dispensable, you know. Everybody loves to eat chicken.

CHICKEN: Why, I oughta . . .

[CHICKEN *starts to go and physically fight with* COW, *but* SHEEP *steps in between the two of them or holds* CHICKEN *back.*]

SHEEP: Stoooooop fighting! Cow, tell us what you heard!

COW: [*stands closer to* SHEEP *than* CHICKEN *to tell the news since she's still a little miffed at* CHICKEN] OK. Now last night, I was grazing near Achan's tent, and I heard his wife crying. She was saying that he shouldn't have stolen the silver and gold. She said nobody needed a Babylonian robe.

CHICKEN: What?

[OFFSTAGE HELPERS *throw directly at all three, and all three animals move at once, either to their right or left, to dodge the rocks.*]

COW: Apparently, Achan and the Israelite army destroyed Jericho. All went well, but Commander Joshua had told them not to take any gold or silver or anything.

SHEEP: Weird. Aaaaaaaall that treasure, and they couldn't have any? I'd be maaaad.

CHICKEN: Now what would a sheep do with gold and silver?

SHEEP: I could have goooooold and silver if I wanted goooooold and silver.

CHICKEN: What would you buy—a wool coat? Ha ha ha ha ha! Get it? A wool coat? 'Cause what would a sheep do with a wool coat? I crack myself up! Ha ha ha!

COW: Look out! Incoming!

[OFFSTAGE HELPERS *throw several paper wads at* SHEEP, *but* COW *pushes* SHEEP *out of the way.*]

SHEEP: Thaaaaat was close!

COW: You're telling me! Now moooooooove over and watch my back! Their aim is getting better. Now where was I? Oh yeah. The people weren't supposed to take the treasure because it was set aside as an offering to God. God gave them the whole city. It's not a lot to ask them to just leave the gold and silver for him.

SHEEP: Yeah, I guess you're riiiiiiiiiiight.

CHICKEN: So Achan took stuff anyway?

COW: Yes. He told his wife that he'd hidden it under the tent and no one would know. But God knew. God talked to Joshua and said that he was angry at Israel because they had ignored his command.

CHICKEN: Way to go, Achan—get everybody in trouble!

COW: So yesterday Joshua told everyone that today was going to be an assembly—God told Joshua to gather the people and then God would point out who sinned. That's why Achan's wife was so upset last night. She knew Achan's stealing spree was going to be found out.

SHEEP: Again, whyyyyy are *we* involved?

COW: God said Achan broke the covenant, so he had to be destroyed. Now Achan's whole family and all his stuff and even his animals—us—get destroyed with him.

SHEEP: You mean, they want to KIIIIIIILL us?

CHICKEN: Duh. What'd you think this was, a friendly game of dodge-rock?

SHEEP: Well, I just thouuuuuuught . . .

COW: Chicken, be nice. Sheep are dumb animals.

CHICKEN: Yeah. They're nothing compared to chickens. It's well known that we're a higher class of animal.

[OFFSTAGE HELPERS begin to throw paper wads, building to pummel CHICKEN and cut him off mid-sentence.]

CHICKEN: Like I always said, the smart species just has a special place in—

[CHICKEN yells and falls to the ground, unconscious.]

COW: *[walks over and looks at the unconscious CHICKEN]* Hmmmm . . . I bet he *does* tastes like chicken!

OFFSTAGE HELPERS: *[step out from offstage, holding hidden paper wads behind their backs; one person or both can say this line]* No actual animals were maimed in this production.

[OFFSTAGE HELPERS then throw the paper wads hidden behind their backs at the audience; actors playing the animals can pick up paper wads from onstage and join in the fun as well.]

Use this parody of a political campaign commercial to retell the
biblical narrative of Jehoshaphat and his leadership skills and
discuss how we can use our own authority responsibly.

2 Chronicles 19:4-10

poster that says "Jehoshaphat—he's all that!" or "Jehoshaphat—
he's where it's at!" or some other clever slogan
suits for JEHOSHAPHAT and PREACHER
robes for JUDGES (could use graduation robes or something similar)
Bible
(optional) spotlight

ANNOUNCER—offstage voice only
KING JEHOSHAPHAT

CROWD—three or four people

JUDGES—two or three people

PREACHER

ANNOUNCER remains offstage and speaks through microphone or loudly for audience to hear. Three scenes will be set up across the stage and will be frozen—the CROWD should be frozen in mid-cheer (with the poster out of view), the JUDGES should be frozen with arms crossed, looking mad, and the PREACHER is frozen looking into an open Bible. JEHOSHAPHAT will go interact with each group of people, who will unfreeze at that moment and go back to being frozen in action once the scene is done. If you have access to a spotlight, you may wish to utilize it to focus on each scene in turn. CROWD is dressed in normal clothes, JUDGES should have on robes, PREACHER and JEHOSHAPHAT both wear suits. Begin with JEHOSHAPHAT standing center stage, smiling as ANNOUNCER describes him.

ANNOUNCER: These are challenging times for our nation of Judah. These times require strong leadership. King Jehoshaphat has proven that he cares about *all* of the people of Judah. Unlike others in Jerusalem who spend their days isolated from the rest of the country, Jehoshaphat is a true man of the people.

[JEHOSHAPHAT steps over to the first group of people, the CROWD. CROWD is excited as JEHOSHAPHAT speaks to them. One person in CROWD holds up the poster as JEHOSHAPHAT speaks.]

JEHOSHAPHAT: Now is the time for the people of this land to remember what we stand for! Now is the time to return to the God of our fathers!

[CROWD cheers loudly in response, then freezes again as ANNOUNCER begins. As ANNOUNCER speaks, JEHOSHAPHAT walks over to JUDGES, who are currently frozen.]

ANNOUNCER: Here is a man not afraid to be seen in Beersheba and the hill country of Ephraim. Here is a man who is not willing to let the message of the Lord stay in Jerusalem. Here is a man whose has held rallies in areas many kings have never visited. There he stirred hearts and renewed the vision of ordinary people in this land. But this compassionate man has shown himself to be a tough-minded reformer. Jehoshaphat has taken on the corruption that too often infects politics. Our king has surrounded himself with men of integrity.

[As JEHOSHAPHAT speaks to JUDGES, at least one of the JUDGES appears defiant and angry, while at least one of the JUDGES appears convicted and changed.]

JEHOSHAPHAT: And I tell you, judges of the fortified cities, if you wish to serve in this administration, you must know that with the Lord our God there is not injustice or partiality or bribery!

[JUDGES freeze again as ANNOUNCER begins. As ANNOUNCER speaks, JEHOSHAPHAT walks over to PREACHER, who is currently frozen. PREACHER is reading an open Bible.]

ANNOUNCER: But most of all, support for Jehoshaphat means a return to the values that made this country great. Once again, our legal system uses God's Word as the basis for establishing right and wrong.

[As JEHOSHAPHAT speaks, he looks over PREACHER's shoulder and points into the Bible.]

JEHOSHAPHAT: In every case that comes before our courts, respect the Lord! Warn every litigant not to sin against the Lord God of Judah!

[PREACHER freezes again as ANNOUNCER begins. As ANNOUNCER speaks, JEHOSHAPHAT walks back to center stage.]

ANNOUNCER: In times like this we need a compassionate, bold, and reverent leader. We need to reelect Jehoshaphat as king of Judah!

JEHOSHAPHAT: *[smiling big]* I'm King Jehoshaphat, and I approve this message.

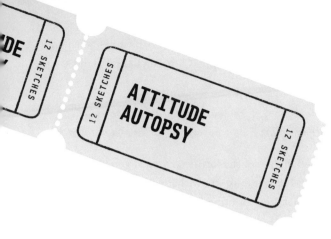

Use this parody of *CSI* (and similar shows) to retell the biblical
narrative of Haman and discuss how selfishness leads to disaster.

Esther 5 and 7

long table
white sheet
lab coat for CASEY
(optional) lab gloves
trench coat for HEATHROW
suit for HAMAN
(optional) more props to decorate the stage like a forensic lab

CASEY—forensic specialist, excited to share the information learned on
the job; can be male or female

HEATHROW—chief investigator; male

HAMAN—male nonspeaking role; pretends to be dead body

CASEY is wearing a lab coat, and HEATHROW is wearing a trench coat. Both enter the stage talking together, with CASEY leading HEATHROW into the lab. HAMAN (dressed in a suit) is lying on a table on another part of the stage, with a sheet covering him. He remains still, as if dead, the entire skit.

CASEY: *[says this line as HEATHROW is following him onstage]* Hello, Heathrow. Come on into my workspace. So who brings you to my lab today?

HEATHROW: Government official, Casey. Big muckety-muck. Gettin' a lot of heat from upstairs on this one.

CASEY: Aaah, yes. We'd be talking about Prime Minister Haman over here. This way . . .

[CASEY leads HEATHROW over to HAMAN's body on the table and pulls back the sheet covering HAMAN. The two stand behind the table to look over HAMAN.]

HEATHROW: Yep. That's our guy. Can't figure out the fuss about this one. Cause of death seems pretty obvious to me.

CASEY: By that I assume you mean this stab wound that goes all the way through his chest.

HEATHROW: Well, sure! The guy was found impaled, hanging from a 75-foot-high gallows!

CASEY: So you assume *that* was the cause of Haman's death?

HEATHROW: Well, yeah! That seems obvious.

CASEY: But obviously *wrong*, Heathrow.

HEATHROW: *[surprised]* What?! What are you trying to tell me?

CASEY: Just that Haman's fate was sealed long before he was hanged from that gallows.

HEATHROW: So whatcha got to show me?

CASEY: Take a look at his right hand.

[HEATHROW picks up the lifeless right hand of HAMAN. HAMAN should have his hand clenched in a fist.]

HEATHROW: Looks abnormally strong. Feels heavy and solid, as if it were made out of metal.

CASEY: Very good. There's actually iron in there. What else do you notice?

HEATHROW: It appears to be tightly clenched—as if Haman was desperately trying to hold on to something.

[HEATHROW lays HAMAN's hand back down on table.]

CASEY: That's right. A condition all too common among some in middle-level leadership positions.

HEATHROW: What condition?

CASEY: It's called power-grab-osis, Heathrow.

HEATHROW: Which is?

CASEY: The intense desire to control others. To rule with an iron fist.

HEATHROW: That doesn't sound deadly to me.

CASEY: Not at first, maybe. But power-grab-osis is progressive. It continues to get worse and worse.

HEATHROW: So how bad did Haman have it?

CASEY: This is obviously an advanced case. It may have started out as just a desire to do a good job. But somebody really set him off.

HEATHROW: How's that?

CASEY: *[animated while describing the situation, using big arm movements, etc.]* Probably someone who reacted to Haman's unreasonable demands and showed some resistance. In this case power-grab-osis causes a person to become almost obsessed with control. Everything has to be *his* way. Everyone has to bow to *his* authority. Eventually the infectious attitude grows. We will see more than an iron fist. *[gestures toward HAMAN's whole body]* The whole person becomes hardened . . . unfeeling . . . inflexible.

HEATHROW: Wow.

CASEY: But there's more, Heathrow.

HEATHROW: Go on.

CASEY: When I did the autopsy, I found something else.

HEATHROW: What?

CASEY: *[taps on HAMAN's chest where his heart would be]* His heart was very small. And hardened. We call it ego-toxic shock.

HEATHROW: Ego-toxic shock?

CASEY: *[again, animated in the description]* That's right. The victim's power goes to his head. He starts to believe that he has done something to earn his power. His ego grows. His heart shrinks. There's just enough room in there for him—no one else.

HEATHROW: Is it painful?

CASEY: Not as much for the patient as for those around him.

HEATHROW: How so?

CASEY: A person with ego-toxic shock is totally self-absorbed. Everything is all about *him*. *He's* got the most important job. *He* knows the most important people. *He* gets invited to the hottest social events.

HEATHROW: Wow. This is interesting stuff! Anything else?

CASEY: Here, at the base of Haman's skull. Take a look right there . . . at that bundle of nerves.

[CASEY turns HAMAN's head over so that they are looking at the back of his neck.]

HEATHROW: *[reaching out to touch the back of HAMAN's neck at the base of his head]* Right there?

CASEY: Don't touch! They're still hot!

HEATHROW: What's hot?

CASEY: His nerves. He has enlarged vengeous nerve syndrome.

HEATHROW: What does that mean?

CASEY: EVN syndrome we call EVeN for short.

Heathrow: Like *get even?*

Casey: *[very excited now]* Exactly, Heathrow! You *have* been paying attention! EVeN causes the patient to seek revenge at all costs.

Heathrow: All costs? What do you mean?

Casey: *[animated again]* A patient is capable of unbelievable cruelty. He might cut off someone's hand if he were suspected of stealing. Or slaughter every inhabitant of a village if he had a quarrel with one of its citizens.

Heathrow: Talk about overkill!

Casey: Well said. And Haman had it bad. He's dead but still hot under the collar! And revenge never cools the rage, only increases it.

Heathrow: So Haman here was doomed before he went to the gallows.

Casey: Exactly!

Heathrow: Let me get this straight. You're telling me that Haman's death started because of his state of mind?

Casey: You got it! And you know what they say.

Heathrow: What's that?

Casey: Attitudes are contagious.

Heathrow: Yeah. And this one could kill you.

HIGH STAKES

12 SKETCHES

Use this skit to retell the biblical narrative of Job's suffering and
discuss the emotions we go through when we are suffering.

Job 19:1-29
Job 23:1-17

15 signs/pieces of paper (big enough to be read by audience but
small enough for one person to hold all 15) with the name of
each racehorse prominently written on a separate sign:

- Heavy Groaning
- Where Is God
- Injured Faith
- Prayer for Acquittal
- Absent Savior
- Invisible Redeemer
- Tested Spirit

- Treasured Words
- Sense of Justice
- Fear of Fickleness
- Terror of the Almighty
- Who Do You Think You Are
- That's Not Fair
- Hope in Darkness
- Blinded by Pain

microphone

piece of paper

(optional) fedora or similar era hat for ANNOUNCER

ANNOUNCER—the only speaking role in this skit, reading all lines; uses the cadence and tone of a horse race announcer

SIGN HOLDER—nonspeaking role; holds all signs with horse names and must display each at the proper time

JOB—nonspeaking role; watches the race and emulates the emotion that each horse name describes

CROWD—nonspeaking roles; as many as you want; react to the horse race, cheering and being disappointed at different times

The names of the horses in this skit represent the different emotions JOB faced throughout his time of suffering. The ANNOUNCER should use a fun tone and cadence like that of a typical race announcer, but he must be sure to enunciate the names of each horse clearly. (ANNOUNCER may wear an old-time hat to represent race announcers in days of yore!)

On stage the ANNOUNCER should be standing with a microphone. ANNOUNCER should appear as if watching a race and enthusiastically telling the audience the location of each horse.

Beside the ANNOUNCER will stand the SIGN HOLDER. The SIGN HOLDER must be sure the stack of signs is in the correct order, with the first horse name on top through the last horse name on the bottom. The SIGN HOLDER

will hold the stack of signs but keep them hidden from view until the race begins. Once the race begins, the SIGN HOLDER will hold up the stack of signs in front of his/her chest with the names facing outward, revealing the first horse name to the audience. Once ANNOUNCER says that horse name, SIGN HOLDER should drop that sign on the floor so that, behind it, the next horse name is revealed. The SIGN HOLDER will keep showing then dropping the signs throughout the race. A couple of times the SIGN HOLDER will reveal two sign names at once when two horses are neck and neck. Make sure the ANNOUNCER and SIGN HOLDER practice this timing together to set a good pace.

Beside the SIGN HOLDER should stand JOB and the CROWD. As the race is run, JOB and the CROWD should react. When a positive named horse takes the lead, JOB should be happy; but when a negative named horse takes the lead, he should be disappointed. The CROWD can be happy and disappointed at different times, as if they are cheering for different horses. Both JOB and the CROWD should be looking and pointing and reacting to one another as if watching a race before them.

ANNOUNCER: Now we come to the final race of today's schedule here at Tribulation Track on the outskirts of Uz. This race is called the High Stakes, and the name couldn't be more appropriate. The horse that goes on to win this race will determine the future of its owner.

[As ANNOUNCER describes JOB in the next few lines, JOB can wave to the audience and to the CROWD, trying to look confident but looking somewhat nervous and a little sad.]

It's going to be a rough race for Job today. He is the owner of many of these thoroughbreds out here. Once a successful businessman, Job has fallen into treacherous circumstances. This race is a last-ditch effort to reclaim his livelihood. If all his horses fail today, it could mean the end for Job.

The track condition is officially designated as "sloppy" as race time approaches. Storms of trouble and suffering have turned this dirt into a muddy mess. These conditions can be very difficult on the most spirited contenders, as we've seen all too many times before.

[JOB and CROWD look excited as they anticipate the start.]

Ladies and gentlemen . . . the horses are at the starting gates . . . and
THEY'RE OFF!

*[Sign Holder now hold the signs in front of his/her chest, displaying the first
name, Heavy Groaning, to the audience, then drops the sign to show the
next one. And so on.]*

Heavy Groaning takes an early lead with **Where Is God** in close pursuit.
Oh no! **Injured Faith** appears to be limping along on the outside! But
what a courageous showing he's making! And **Prayer for Acquittal** is
right by his side!

But here comes **Absent Savior** making a challenge. And **Invisible
Redeemer**, who's close beside him, seems to be overtaking both **Injured
Faith** and **Prayer for Acquittal**. These horses are really taking a beating
out there!

*[Since Sign Holder has already dropped Absent Savior and Invisible
Redeemer, no need to worry about those; just leave them on the floor. As
Announcer gets to the names Treasured Words and Sense of Justice, Sign
Holder should hold both up at the same time as they race close together.]*

But what's this? Out of the middle of the pack comes **Tested Spirit**!
It's **Tested Spirit** confronting **Absent Savior**, as **Treasured Words**
and **Sense of Justice** begin to make their moves. **Treasured Words**
overcomes **Invisible Redeemer**, and **Sense of Justice** is coming on
strong!

*[Sign Holder should now drop both Treasured Words and Sense of Justice
signs.]*

But the race is far from over, folks! **Fear of Fickleness** is determined to make a
race of it. **Terror of the Almighty** is moving on the inside, followed closely
by **Who Do You Think You Are** and **That's Not Fair**.

*[For this final section of the race, Sign Holder should hold up both Hope in
Darkness and Blinded by Pain signs as they are neck and neck to the finish.
Sign Holder should raise and lower each one as they take turns taking the lead.]*

Coming down the homestretch it's **Hope in Darkness**. **Blinded by Pain**
pulls even with **Hope in Darkness**. It's **Hope in Darkness** . . . **Blinded
by Pain** . . . **Hope in Darkness** . . . Ladies and gentlemen, these two
horses are neck and neck. It's **Blinded by Pain** . . . **Hope in Darkness**
. . . **Blinded by Pain** . . . as the finish line approaches quickly. **Hope in
Darkness** . . . **Blinded by Pain** . . . **Hope in Darkness** . . . They cross
the line, and . . . it looks like we have a photo finish!

*[JOB and CROWD look excited at the finish but then confused as they wonder
which horse truly won.]*

It's going to take a judge's decision on this one! *What* a race! What a *race*!
What—a—race!

THE JOB FAIR

12 SKETCHES

>>> PURPOSE:

Use this skit to retell the biblical narrative of Ezekiel's call from
God and discuss how one person can make a difference in the
world by being a modern-day watchman and calling others
to God.

>>> PORTION OF SCRIPTURE:

Ezekiel 33:1-11

>>> PROPS:

three or four desks or tables
poster that says "God Jobs"
tape
papers, pamphlets, etc.

>>> PEOPLE:

PRINCIPAL—male or female
ZEKE—male, a modern-day Ezekiel
RECRUITER—male or female

EXTRAS—you'll need one person per job fair table to be the job representatives and several extras milling around as students

Stage should be set up to look like a job fair. Have several tables at various places across the stage with one prominently placed front and center. The main table should have the "God Jobs" poster taped to the front of it. Each table should have some papers on it as you'd see at a job fair. One EXTRA should stand behind each table while RECRUITER stands behind the "God Jobs" table. Other EXTRAS and ZEKE mill around as students going from table to table and pretending to talk to the people behind the tables and picking up the pamphlets. PRINCIPAL enters and says line as an announcement to everyone onstage.

PRINCIPAL: Welcome to the annual Waters-Babylon High School job fair. We welcome all of our exhibitors from both inside and outside our community and encourage all students to carefully consider these fine opportunities that can put you on the track toward a bright future!

[After PRINCIPAL speaks, he/she can walk around and pretend to talk with EXTRAS. Can eventually leave stage if desired.]

ZEKE: *[approaches the God Jobs table and looks at the sign with some confusion]* Your sign here says "God Jobs." Did you mean to write "*Good* Jobs"?

RECRUITER: No, the sign is right. "God Jobs." Our slogan is, "Seeking those who will change the world for God!"

ZEKE: Change the world? Sounds like more of a job than one person can handle.

RECRUITER: True, but everyone available is necessary. We always have plenty of openings. What's your name, young man?

ZEKE: *[shakes RECRUITER's hand as he speaks]* Ezekiel. Call me Zeke.

RECRUITER: Well, Zeke, I can tell you that we need you at God Jobs.

ZEKE: I guess it's worth looking into. What kind of positions do you have open right now?

RECRUITER: Well, we are looking for a lifeguard at Eternal Peril Beach.

[RECRUITER *hands* ZEKE *a pamphlet.* ZEKE *looks at it and then says next line.*]

ZEKE: A lifeguard?

RECRUITER: [*animated, really selling the job description*] Every day people purposely plunge into Eternal Peril. The tide is so dangerous that it quickly draws folks under. We need to post a lifeguard to warn people not to dive into those waters.

ZEKE: Wow, that sounds like quite a task. What if they don't listen?

RECRUITER: Sadly, some people won't. But the owner of the beach isn't hiring you to physically restrain someone from jumping into Eternal Peril.

ZEKE: Oh really?

RECRUITER: No. He doesn't work that way. If you are posted there and you don't warn someone, then *you* are responsible. But if people ignore your warnings, that's their *own* choice.

ZEKE: That sounds kind of heartless. The owner of the beach has this dangerous property, and he wants to hire *one guy* to keep people out?

RECRUITER: [*at this point can walk around to the front of the table while talking to* ZEKE] Oh no! The owner has posted lifeguards up and down the beach. His written regulations are well known to people in the area. He has consistently warned people of the dangers found there. He has fenced off the area for decades. But . . .

ZEKE: [*finishing the sentence*] . . . people still dive in.

RECRUITER: Sadly, that's true.

ZEKE: There has to be more that can be done!

RECRUITER: What do you suggest?

ZEKE: I don't know, but doesn't the owner care that people are dying?

RECRUITER: He does, and it breaks his heart. People not only dive into dangerous waters, but they do so with weights on their feet!

ZEKE: Weights?

RECRUITER: Yes, they dive in with all of their useless belongings that they think will bring them pleasure. And those things only make them sink faster.

ZEKE: And this happens often?

RECRUITER: Far too often, I'm afraid. The owner is constantly urging these stubborn ones to turn back. He certainly takes no pleasure in anyone dying there!

ZEKE: Yet people still jump in and they still die. Why?

RECRUITER: Perhaps it's because we need more lifeguards. The owner cares. Those who die have the choice not to. That's why we need people like you on the job. All that we are requiring of you is to issue the warning. *[puts a hand on ZEKE's shoulder]* C'mon Zeke. Can't we count on you?

>>> **PURPOSE:**

Use this parody of an extreme sports show to retell the biblical
narrative of Peter walking on water and discuss how we can
deal with doubt.

>>> **PORTION OF SCRIPTURE:**

Matthew 14:22-33

>>> **PROPS:**

microphone
swim trunks and T-shirt or wetsuit
(optional) surfboard

>>> **PEOPLE:**

GABE ANGELO—sports announcer
SIMON PETER—California surfer version of the disciple

GABE has a microphone and is interviewing PETER. PETER is dressed in either a T-shirt and swim trunks or in a wetsuit. If a surfboard is available, PETER can be holding it. As PETER describes his experience of walking on the water throughout the skit, he can be overly dramatic in his physical movements to make his descriptions come alive!

GABE: Welcome to AXN, Ancient Extreme Sports Network. I'm Gabe Angelo. Today we are here on the shores of the beautiful Sea of Galilee. I'm talking to Simon Peter. Pete is the owner and founder of Simon Peter's School of Surf. Welcome, Pete.

PETER: Thanks, dude.

GABE: Pete, it's great to talk to a true innovator in X-sports. Today we want to talk about your unique contribution to the sport. I'm talking, of course, about the invention of boardless surfing.

PETER: Well, Gabe, you don't need a board when you're surfin' with the Lord!

GABE: We know that's your motto. But when it comes to boardless surfing, I think it's safe to say that we are all grommets—you know, beginners. Can you give us some basic tips?

PETER: Sure, Gabe, my man. The first step is be chill and overcome your fear.

GABE: That sounds like a tall order. How did you conquer the fear that kept you off the waves?

PETER: *[can use dramatic physical movements as he describes the scene]* It all happened that night when my bros, the other disciples, and I started to cross this sea without Jesus. We were on dawn patrol, dude. You know, it was like o'dark-thirty in the morning. All of a sudden, a storm came up. Before long, the whole sea was totally blown out—waves coming from every direction at once. We were like, "Whoa!"

GABE: So you were scared?

PETER: You think! The whole boat was in the spin cycle, dude! As if it couldn't get worse, we see this *thing*—this ghostlike thing walking over the surface of the water!

GABE: You're not telling me ghost stories, are you, Pete?

PETER: But it wasn't a ghost, man. It was Jesus! And the first thing he said was, "Don't be afraid!"

GABE: That sounds easier said than done!

PETER: You'd think so. But just hearing his voice . . . Just hearing his calming voice, man . . . Remembering that helps me conquer fear when I'm out there.

GABE: Allow Jesus to take away your fear . . . I see. What other advice to you have?

PETER: Dude, the next thing I learned that night was to accept the challenge.

GABE: How's that?

PETER: When I saw Jesus riding the waves without a board, I was like, "I gotta be out there too!" He turned to me and said, "Come."

GABE: So you jumped out of the boat?

PETER: [physically demonstrates being on the water as he speaks] It was awesome, dude! I kept my eye on the Lord. I didn't look at my feet at all. I was stoked! It felt like I was toes-on-the-nose of a short board! Gnarly waves were breakin' all around us, and I was rippin', dude!

GABE: Wow! You make it sound easy!

PETER: Whoa! Not so fast! It was and it wasn't. That's the last thing you gotta know before you go boardless surfing.

GABE: Which is?

PETER: Don't be afraid to wipe out.

GABE: But it sounded like you did so well.

PETER: I did. Until I started getting my head into it. I said to myself, "Dude, you can't do this. It's impossible!" I started to doubt, and I took my eyes off Jesus.

GABE: And . . . ?

PETER: [pretends to crash into the water] Wipeout! I totally ate it, dude.

GABE: What happened?

PETER: Jesus grabbed me and took me back on the boat. He let me have it for not trusting in him. But it was cool, you know.

GABE: Why?

PETER: 'Cause, he was still going to be with me. Jesus will be there to pick me up, like every time I wipe out.

GABE: Pete, thanks for joining us today. Do you have any final words for the folks out there?

PETER: You know the motto, dude.

GABE: Sure do.

GABE AND PETER: *[PETER can be giving the "hang ten" hand sign.]* YOU DON'T NEED A BOARD WHEN YOU'RE SURFIN' WITH THE LORD!

GABE: *[to audience]* You heard it here first! And good-night from all of us at AXN.

REAL WORLD:
JERICHO

12 SKETCHES

12 SKETCHES

12 SKETCHES

>>> PURPOSE:

Use this parody of *The Real World* to retell the biblical narrative of
Bartimaeus and discuss how God wants us to seek his mercy.

>>> PORTION OF SCRIPTURE:

Mark 10:46-52

>>> PROPS:

video camera on tripod
chair
sunglasses for BART

>>> PEOPLE:

NARRATOR—male or female
BARTIMAEUS (BART)—blind and desperate for Jesus
CROWD WOMAN—loud, obviously uneducated and unrefined
DISCIPLE OF JESUS

This is intended to be a commercial for an upcoming episode of a show that parodies MTV's The Real World. *As on* The Real World, *characters speak into the camera that's set up (no camera person running it), like a video diary.* NARRATOR *should be off to one side of the stage during the entire skit.*

On the other side of the stage, set up the video camera in front of a chair so that all the other characters can speak their lines to the camera as if recording their thoughts. Since there would be too many entrances and exits to stage, keep BARTIMAEUS, CROWD WOMAN, *and* DISCIPLE OF JESUS *onstage, behind the video camera/chair setup with their backs turned to audience. When it's time for each character to talk, he/she will turn around, sit in chair, and then speak.*

NARRATOR: Find out what happens when people *stop* being polite and *start* getting REAL on *Real World: Jericho.* Next week on *Real World: Jericho* . . . He's known around town as Blind Bartimaeus, but Bart starts seeing things clearly!

BARTIMAEUS: *[wearing sunglasses, turns, sits down on chair, facing camera]* Sorry for the sunglasses. Still getting used to all this light! It was amazing when it happened! You have no idea! I was sitting at the city gates when Jesus came out. People around me told me who he was. I couldn't contain myself!

[As NARRATOR *says next line,* BARTIMAEUS *gets up and stands again with others, back to audience, while* CROWD WOMAN *sits down on chair.]*

NARRATOR: But not everyone was thrilled with the way Bart acted. We'll hear from a woman in the crowd that day.

CROWD WOMAN: I ain't *never* seen the likes of it! The gall of that man! The prophet from Nazareth is an important man. Too important for the likes of a blind guy! But there was Bartimaeus, just a-shoutin' and carryin' on! *[mocking tone]* "Have mercy! Have mercy!" *[harsher tone]* Mercy? *I'd* like to give him a taste of mercy, all right!

[As NARRATOR *says next line,* CROWD WOMAN *gets up and stands again with others, back to audience, while* BARTIMAEUS *sits down again on chair.]*

NARRATOR: Will other people's anger stop Bartimaeus? Not the Bartimaeus we've come to know and love!

BARTIMAEUS: *[chuckling]* People around me told me to shut up, that I was making a fool of myself. I didn't care. I'd heard about Jesus. I knew he was the Son of David, the promised Messiah. The prophet said that Messiah would open the eyes of the blind. I figured, hey, I'm blind. This could work out pretty good for me!

[BARTIMAEUS gets up and stands again with others, back to audience, while CROWD WOMAN sits down again on chair.]

CROWD WOMAN: I don't care what Bartimaeus tells you. It was embarrassin'. I'm surprised Jesus' disciples didn't chase him away! But they didn't.

[As NARRATOR says next line, CROWD WOMAN gets up and stands again with others, back to audience, while DISCIPLE OF JESUS sits down on chair.]

NARRATOR: Bart sure leaves a memorable impression on people, now doesn't he? Even a disciple of Jesus can't get the guy out of his head.

DISCIPLE OF JESUS: Bart sure knew how to get attention. Actually, I was about ready to go calm the guy down a little. But then the Master stopped. Jesus asked me to call Bartimaeus over to him.

[DISCIPLE OF JESUS gets up and stands again with others, back to audience, while BARTIMAEUS sits down again on chair.]

BARTIMAEUS: I think the crowd around me was more shocked than I was! They told me to get up, not to keep Jesus waiting. I barely heard them. I don't know how I did it, but I ran toward his voice. I'm surprised I didn't run into people and knock several of them over! I was there in a flash.

[As NARRATOR says next line, BARTIMAEUS gets up and stands again with others, back to audience, while DISCIPLE OF JESUS sits down again on chair.]

NARRATOR: Bart gets a face-to-face with Jesus. Will he get what he hopes for?

DISCIPLE OF JESUS: A lot of times when people call out for Jesus, they just want attention. Other times they really aren't all that sure of what Jesus can do—or even what they want out of life, for that matter. So Jesus asked Bart a simple question.

[DISCIPLE OF JESUS gets up and stands again with others, back to audience, while BARTIMAEUS sits down again on chair.]

BARTIMAEUS: Jesus asked me what I wanted. Not a hint of hesitation on my part! "I want to see!" I shouted. "The Messiah will give sight to the blind! And here I am!" I guess I was a little bold, but he knew exactly what I wanted.

[BARTIMAEUS gets up and stands again with others, back to audience, while CROWD WOMAN sits down again on chair.]

CROWD WOMAN: I never seen anything like what happened next! I known Bartimaeus for a long time. Always been blind. Always! But in the blink of an eye, that changed. Ha! Blink of an eye! Get it?

[CROWD WOMAN gets up and stands again with others, back to audience, while BARTIMAEUS sits down again on chair.]

BARTIMAEUS: Just like that, I could see! Everything! People! Colors! The bluest of blue skies!

[BARTIMAEUS gets up and stands again with others, back to audience, while DISCIPLE OF JESUS sits down again on chair.]

DISCIPLE OF JESUS: *[chuckles]* And *that* wasn't the last we heard of Bart! He grabbed his coat and followed right along with us. He hasn't been out of Jesus' sight since then! He's been great to have around though. He'd do anything for Jesus. I've never seen such enthusiasm and gratitude. When we get around a crowd, we can't shut him up! He's just got to tell everybody what happened to him.

NARRATOR: We'll check in on Bart and friends in their house in Jericho and see how relationship dynamics change, now that a blind guy can see. All this and more, next week on *Real World: Jericho*. You won't want to miss it!

WHY DO WE NEED TO KNOW THIS?

12 SKETCHES
12 SKETCHES
12 SKETCHES
12 SKETCHES

>>> **PURPOSE:**

Use this skit to retell the biblical narrative of Paul speaking in Athens and discuss why it's important that we know what's going on in the world.

>>> **PORTION OF SCRIPTURE:**

Acts 17:16-34

>>> **PROPS:**

desks
chairs
khakis and dress shirt for PAUL
books
notebooks
pens

>>> **PEOPLE:**

PAUL—the apostle
CHELSEA—student

DEVIN—student

OTHER STUDENTS—nonspeaking roles, as many as you want

Set up the stage like a classroom. There should be a large teacher's desk and then smaller student desks and chairs. Angle the setup so no one's back is to the audience. CHELSEA should sit in the first row, and DEVIN should sit somewhere prominent. Allow OTHER STUDENTS to fill in the class, as many or as few as you want. OTHER STUDENTS have no speaking lines but should react nonverbally to the dialogue. CHELSEA, DEVIN, and OTHER STUDENTS should have some combination of books, notebooks, and pens in front of them. Have PAUL dressed in khakis and a dress shirt and sit on the front of the teacher's desk in a casual pose.

PAUL: Hello, I am your teacher, the apostle Paul. Welcome to the Newtown Christian School current events class. This semester, we will regularly be studying the daily newspaper, broadcast news, news magazines, and similar sources . . .

CHELSEA: *[interrupting with hand raised]* Oooh. Oooh.

PAUL: Ah . . . yes. The young lady in the first row. What is your name, please?

CHELSEA: Hi. I'm Chelsea.

PAUL: Thank you, Chelsea. Now, you appear to have a question?

CHELSEA: Yeah. Do we have to take notes?

PAUL: I would think that would be helpful.

DEVIN: But why? Why do we need to know this?

PAUL: *[addressing DEVIN]* Your name?

DEVIN: I'm Devin, sir. I'm just wondering, when will we ever need all this current events stuff in real life?

PAUL: That's a good question. And it's one I asked many, many years ago. I committed myself to a study of the Scriptures, and I thought that was enough. But is it?

CHELSEA: That's what I've been taught.

PAUL: Let me tell you about a time when I was far away from my home.

When I was in the city of Athens, it was like being in a whole other world. Huge buildings, philosophers discussing the meaning of life on the street corners, idols everywhere . . . I felt a little intimidated.

DEVIN: So what did you do?

PAUL: I studied current events. I watched what was going on around me. The first thing that really hit me was the number of idols in the city.

CHELSEA: We see stuff all the time here in town that doesn't honor God. Why did the idols surprise you?

PAUL: Think about it. Here I was in this intellectual center—a place that claimed to have all the answers. Then I realized all this knowledge didn't satisfy them. They were still looking for spiritual meaning!

DEVIN: I never would have thought about it like that!

PAUL: I started preaching and teaching in the marketplace. There was no shortage of philosophers out there.

DEVIN: Weren't you nervous?

PAUL: I'll have to admit, I was a bit nervous! Fortunately, I had paid attention to currently popular philosophies, so I knew what I was talking about when I had discussions with the Stoic and Epicurean philosophers.

CHELSEA: The Sto-whos and the Epi-whats?!

PAUL: [chuckles a little] The Stoics and Epicureans. The Stoics had kind of a tough street kid philosophy. They thought suffering was a part of life and there was nothing anyone could do to stop it. They thought people should look suffering in the face, shrug their shoulders, and say, "Whatever."

CHELSEA: OK.

PAUL: The Epicureans were more like spoiled rich kid philosophers. They figured life was basically good and full of pleasure. When people didn't get the good things they deserved, they believed it was because someone messed up.

DEVIN: So which one was right?

PAUL: Neither. The Epicureans were wrong: suffering *does* happen, because sin entered the world long ago. But the Stoics are also wrong: sin *won't* last forever, because God arranged for the penalty of sin to be paid through Jesus.

CHELSEA: So what'd they do when you started talking?

PAUL: At first they thought I was just an outsider who wasn't worth listening to! But because I was able to demonstrate that I understood them, they started treating me with some respect. They even invited me to speak at the Areopagus, the gathering of some of their finest philosophers.

DEVIN: Cool.

PAUL: I thought so too. Then I thought, *I'm only going to have a few minutes to get their attention. How will I do it? What will be my opening?*

DEVIN: What'd you say?

PAUL: I remembered my walk around the city again. I noticed something strange while I was studying their city. Most of the idols had specific names on them. But one was simply labeled "To an Unknown God."

CHELSEA: So you used that knowledge to lead into a discussion of Jesus, right? Because our God is that Unknown God who loved them so much that he sent his Son.

PAUL: Now you're seeing my strategy!

DEVIN: OK. I think I get it now. Understanding current events helps us know the questions of people around us so we can give the right answers.

PAUL: Exactly. And that's what we'll be doing as we study current events together this semester. Just as . . .

CHELSEA: *[interrupting again with hand raised]* Oooh. Oooh.

PAUL: Ah . . . yes. Chelsea, do you have another question?

CHELSEA: Yeah. Is this gonna be on the test?

THE LATE, LATE
NIGHT SHOW

12 SKETCHES
12 SKETCHES
12 SKETCHES
12 SKETCHES

Use this parody of a late-night talk show to retell the biblical
narrative of Paul during house arrest and discuss the
opportunities we have to share the good news of Jesus.

Acts 28:17-31

large desk or table
two chairs
suit for CAMERON
sign that says "Applause"
chain, handcuffs, or at least a large rope
two coffee mugs
a couple of pieces of paper
(optional) theme music that sounds like a talk show entrance

STAGEHAND—nonspeaking role

CAMERON O'RYAN—imitating late-night talk show host Conan
O'Brien

PAUL—apostle of Jesus

DECIMUS—nonspeaking role; big and burly Roman guard

*Have a large desk or table set up in the middle of the stage with one chair
behind it and one beside it, facing the audience, as you'd see on a late-
night show for the host and guest. Put one coffee mug on the desk, slightly
toward the end where the guest sits and the papers where CAMERON will sit.
Keep the other coffee mug offstage. If you want to play some theme music
for CAMERON's entrance, play it at the beginning. With or without music,
CAMERON, wearing a suit, should run out onto the stage and wave to the
audience and stop front and center. STAGEHAND is seated near front side of
stage and holds up "Applause" sign to the audience as CAMERON enters, so
that everyone in the audience claps. Keep the "Applause" sign up until he
says a couple of thank-yous. (You may want to talk to some in the audience
beforehand to be sure they clap to get everyone going along with the audience
participation.)*

CAMERON: Thank you. Thank you. Thank you. Really, folks, I know you love
me, but we have a show to do! Hey, everyone, welcome to *The Late, Late
Night Show*. I'm your lovable and dashing host, Cameron O'Ryan!

[STAGEHAND holds up "Applause" sign again to the audience.]

CAMERON: I know, I know. You could applaud all night. Let's get started. We
have a great show tonight! I know I always say that. But it's true! And I'm
so excited about our guest tonight that I'm going to skip my monologue
and go straight to the guest segment. Everyone, please welcome a mover
and shaker of the religious world, Paul of Tarsus!

*[STAGEHAND holds up "Applause" sign to the audience as PAUL and DECIMUS
enter, so that everyone in the audience claps. PAUL and DECIMUS are chained
together, either at the arm or leg. Make the chain long enough so they aren't
too uncomfortable and can remain some distance apart. PAUL should shake*

CAMERON's hand, and then both PAUL and CAMERON should sit in their chairs. DECIMUS should look tough and grumpy with arms crossed and stand behind PAUL's chair, facing the audience.]

PAUL: Thanks, Cameron. I appreciate your introduction, but I'm not much of a mover or a shaker these days, since I'm chained to a Roman soldier. I'm still glad to be here though!

CAMERON: Yeah, I sort of noticed your chain. Does big guy here need a chair or anything?

[As PAUL says his next lines, DECIMUS picks up the coffee mug and pretends to drink the entire thing. He slams it back down, upside down, on the desk and loudly burps.]

PAUL: No, Decimus is pretty self-sufficient. As you can see, he takes just about anything he wants or needs, like your coffee there. *[noticing DECIMUS has drunk the coffee]* Whoops! Sorry about that. He seems to have developed a caffeine addiction.

CAMERON: I *was* going to drink that, but I suppose you don't argue with a guy whose arms are as big as my head. And I have a big head! Hey, that reminds me of a joke . . . Where does a 6-foot, 3-inch legionnaire sit?

[There's a short pause, followed by DECIMUS dumping CAMERON out of his chair and then sitting in it himself. STAGEHAND holds up "Applause" sign to the audience.]

PAUL: Apparently he sits in your chair. Decimus, please, let the nice man back in his seat.

[DECIMUS crosses his arms and growls.]

PAUL: Yes, you can have more coffee.

CAMERON: *[getting up from the floor]* Can somebody get this guy more coffee?

[DECIMUS gets up from the chair. CAMERON sits down in the chair. STAGEHAND runs offstage and grabs the other coffee mug and then hesitantly comes back onstage and hands it to DECIMUS and then quickly heads back to original spot, as if afraid to get too close to DECIMUS.]

CAMERON: Wow! Live television, folks! Anything can happen! Paul, I know everybody wants to know how you can still stir up so much controversy with a guy like *this [gestures to DECIMUS]* hanging around all the time.

[DECIMUS flexes his muscles and looks proud.]

PAUL: Actually, I'm not sure about how much trouble I'm stirring up, but I haven't had any problems preaching the gospel since I got to Rome.

CAMERON: Yes, I got some details from your publicist, Luke, before the interview. *[looks at papers in front of him]*

PAUL: Actually, he's a doctor . . .

CAMERON: Fascinating stuff here . . . stonings, mob scenes, beatings . . . even a shipwreck! What a great story. I suppose you need a bodyguard like Decimus just to keep the paparazzi at bay.

PAUL: No, it's not the paparazzi he has to protect me from. But I *do* need protection.

CAMERON: From whom? A popular guy like you surely doesn't have enemies.

PAUL: Well, if you'd read down to about the end of what Luke has written, *[gestures toward papers in front of CAMERON]* you'd see that I'm really not all that popular with quite a number of Jews around the world.

CAMERON: Maybe *that's* why Decimus drinks all that caffeine! You know, I just heard a few comments from some of the guys on the set before we got started. Seems that they're from Synagogue #118 here in town, and they've been talking about you for the past couple of weeks.

PAUL: That's right. I had a short lecture series there for a few days, but some of the leaders didn't like what I had to say. I have to admit I was ready for a fight from day one, considering that the Jews from Jerusalem have been hounding me the last few years. It turns out that nobody had heard any of the complaints from Jerusalem, so I was able to start from the beginning and share the gospel.

CAMERON: That's pretty impressive that you came prepared for any battle.

PAUL: Well, when you have such an important message and so many different people to hear it and react to it, it's best to be prepared for all situations.

CAMERON: I understand you've had a change of venue?

PAUL: Not exactly. You see, I am actually a prisoner under house arrest. So while Decimus here does go with me wherever I need to go, I typically stay at home. Besides, the crowd I had coming to hear me talk about Jesus was pretty big. They came over to the place I'm renting right now. I had to talk with them outside because everyone couldn't fit indoors!

CAMERON: Does your landlord mind the crowd?

PAUL: Well, I have had some heated disagreements with a few people. But my guests have overall been well-behaved. And some of the Jews began to believe and have been coming back, bringing others with them to hear about Jesus. I wouldn't be surprised if they keep coming for several years!

CAMERON: You know, that's generous. I'd never want that many people to come to my house! We have to go to commercial break now, but would you stick around and share more with us?

PAUL: Actually, Decimus gets cranky if he doesn't get his sleep, so we'd better head back. But if you or anyone else wants to stop by, my door's always open!

CAMERON: Sounds great. There you have it folks: Paul, man of this world and the next. Stop by his place anytime and check out what he has to say!

[DECIMUS leans over and whispers to CAMERON.]

CAMERON: *[to DECIMUS]* Sure. *[to audience]* Decimus says, if you come, bring coffee!

[STAGEHAND holds up "Applause" sign to the audience.]

Use this parody of *So You Think You Can Dance* to restate biblical teaching about moral purity from Paul's letter to the church at Thessalonica.

1 Thessalonians 4:1-8

stool
small table
two chairs
(optional) props on the table that would be in a restaurant, such as silverware, plates, and glasses

CAMI—enthusiastic host of the show (optional: British accent to imitate the *So You Think You Can Dance* host)
AMBER—small-town girl

WILL—smooth and suave and tries hard to be slick

JANELLE—flirty and dangerous

MARCUS—solid, down-to-earth, dependable

PAUL—apostle of Jesus

Contestants are all standing in a row, with a little space between them, center stage, facing the audience. They should be in this order: AMBER, WILL, JANELLE, MARCUS. CAMI begins by standing off to one side, talking to the audience. PAUL is on the opposite side of the stage, sitting on a stool. The table and two chairs are set up as if it's a restaurant—but behind the contestants, unseen by audience.

CAMI: *[enthusiastic]* Welcome to the final episode of *So You Think You Can Date.* I'm your host, Cami. For weeks now we've watched as contestants were paired off and placed in dating situations to see how they acted. You, our devoted audience, have chosen which contestants performed the best each week on specific dating elements. Now we're down to the last two couples with the final elimination to be announced tonight. Let's meet our final four contestants: Amber, Will, Janelle, and Marcus!

[Contestants smile and wave to audience.]

CAMI: In last week's episode, the two couples were in their final dating situations. This date tested one of the hardest dating elements to master—purity. But the contestants did *not* know that they were being judged on purity. And for some of them, their behavior showed it. After last week's show, you cast your votes for the best female and male—the winners of *So You Think You Can Date.* Who did America choose? We'll find out soon. But first, let's learn more about the final competition.

[CAMI walks over and stands by each contestant as she speaks to him/her. CAMI starts by standing beside AMBER.]

CAMI: First up is Amber. She quickly captured audience attention with her small-town, down-home attitude. During last week's date, she showed the same genuineness that she has displayed week after week on the show. Amber, did you anticipate that you would be judged on purity?

AMBER: No, ma'am, I did not.

CAMI: So you didn't alter your behavior in any way?

AMBER: No. I just acted the way I always do. I'm a lady, and I expect to be treated like one.

[As she speaks, CAMI moves over to stand beside WILL.]

CAMI: Good for you. Amber's date last week was Will. Will has kept a suave and macho persona this entire competition. Will, how did you react once you found out that you were being judged on purity last week?

WILL: Yikes! That's all I can say. But you know, if the audience didn't vote me as the winner, maybe you and I can go out sometime, Cami.

[WILL tries to put his arm around CAMI, but as she speaks, she quickly moves away to stand by JANELLE.]

CAMI: Um, no thanks. Moving on. We have Janelle. Janelle, you were labeled as a flirt, and you seemed to be particularly interested in flirting with Marcus last week.

JANELLE: What can I say, Cami? When you've got an outgoing personality, people will always judge you. I thought Marcus was cute, and I wasn't ashamed to let him know.

[As she speaks, CAMI moves over to stand beside MARCUS.]

CAMI: Yes, we saw. Finally, there's Marcus. Marcus has remained steady in the voting polls the whole competition. He's the guy every mom wants her daughter to date. Marcus, what did you think of last week's date?

MARCUS: Honestly, I knew Janelle's reputation going into it. But she definitely put the pressure on more than I anticipated.

CAMI: OK. We'll find out which guy and which girl the audience chose as the winners of this season's *So You Think You Can Date*. But first, let's talk to our judge, Paul, the apostle!

[PAUL smiles and waves to audience as CAMI walks over to him. All four contestants move over to stand on the opposite side of the stage, revealing the table center stage.]

CAMI: Paul, what is your take on last week's date?

PAUL: Well, Cami, last week's date was crucial to this contest. The four contestants were being judged on purity—a quality that can express the essence of a person's character. The results were *quite* revealing.

CAMI: Let's have a recap of last week's dates, and you tell us what you observed, Paul.

[As PAUL describes the date in his next lines, WILL and AMBER walk over to the table. WILL pulls out AMBER's chair for her as PAUL describes it and then pantomimes talking to AMBER, trying to impress her. Then as PAUL says his "schmooze" line, WILL leans across the table and whispers something to AMBER, and she pretends to slap him.]

PAUL: All right. Well, first Will took Amber out to a nice restaurant. He starts off good, holding the door for Amber and pulling her chair out for her. But when they begin dinner conversation, Will goes downhill from there. By the end of appetizers, Will was already trying to schmooze Amber, but he did so in a vulgar manner. *[says next line after AMBER pretends to slap WILL]* Whoa! Will had that one coming! I won't repeat his exact words—no need to expose our audience to his impure language.

CAMI: Wow, I'll bet that was tough for Amber to endure. *[walks over to the table where AMBER and WILL are still sitting and stands between them]* Amber, how did you feel?

AMBER: I was appalled! I've never heard such things coming from a guy. I'll admit that I haven't dated much, but I can't imagine the guy friends in my youth group ever talking to girls that way!

PAUL: That was definitely evident. As you could see, Amber kept her dignity and firmly told Will that he should not speak to her in that manner. In fact, the date was supposed to continue to a coffee shop after dinner, but Amber declined and asked for a cab to take her home. I give strong points to Amber for that move.

CAMI: *[turns to look at WILL]* Will, do you have anything to say?

WILL: Amber, maybe you're just sheltered. I didn't say or do anything that the guys in the locker room don't talk about at school. I didn't think a girl existed who's as innocent as you! I don't know what you were expecting, but *this* is what dating is like where I come from. I was fine that you went home. I've got other girls I can call who will see things my way. And Cami . . . *[tries to reach for CAMI's hand]*

CAMI: *[interrupts]* I said *no*, Will.

[CAMI walks back over to PAUL as she says the next line. At the same time, WILL and AMBER get up and move back to the other side of the stage while JANELLE and MARCUS take their places.]

CAMI: OK, Paul. Now let's get your thoughts on Janelle and Marcus's date.

[As PAUL describes the date, JANELLE does the actions he describes: tries to grab MARCUS's hand and scoots her chair around the table, closer to MARCUS. She continues trying to play with MARCUS's hair or touch his arm or look seductive. MARCUS tries to shift away from JANELLE and tries to avoid looking at her for very long.]

PAUL: You can see that Marcus begins the night with polite conversation, trying to get to know Janelle as a person. But you'll notice right away that Janelle tries to reach for Marcus's hand and sit closer to him to make physical contact with him. Janelle does not appear interested in conversation at all. Not the actions I'd expect from a young lady focused on purity.

[CAMI walks over to the table and stands by JANELLE.]

CAMI: Janelle, what do you think of Paul's impression of you?

JANELLE: I never said I *was* focused on purity! Even if I'd known that the last competition was about something so stuffy as purity, I still would've hit on Marcus. I don't pass up an opportunity to try and be close to a good-looking guy!

CAMI: Strong words, Janelle. *[moves to stand by MARCUS]* Marcus, what were you thinking on the date?

MARCUS: Cami, I've always tried to be a gentleman. I was raised in a Christian home, and my parents taught me to honor women. But Janelle wasn't making it easy. I'll be honest—she is *very* nice looking! She *was* tempting me to stray from pure thoughts. But I kept asking God to help me do the right thing and just get me through the date.

CAMI: *[moves back over to PAUL]* Well, you stayed strong. Paul, give us your final assessment of the night.

[As PAUL says his next line, JANELLE and MARCUS get up from the table, and all four contestants move to stand center stage in the places they stood at the beginning of the skit.]

PAUL: If the voters did their job, they will have chosen Amber and Marcus as the two teens who demonstrated purity on their dates. Those two should be chosen as the winners of this season's *So You Think You Can Date*.

CAMI: Thanks, Paul. *[to audience, smiling]* After this commercial break, we'll reveal the final results and find out if the audience agreed with Paul on his choices for the winners. Stay tuned!

PAUL'S JOB INTERVIEW

PA'
I

>>> PURPOSE:

Use this skit to restate the biblical description of Paul's life change and discuss how we are pardoned by Jesus from our sins and have been given salvation.

>>> PORTION OF SCRIPTURE:

1 Timothy 1:12-17

>>> PROPS:

long table
four chairs
several pieces of paper for each interviewer
pen for each interviewer
business clothes for DYLAN, KAYLA, and CONNOR
khakis and dress shirt for PAUL

>>> PEOPLE:

DYLAN—search committee member and interviewer
KAYLA—search committee member and interviewer

CONNOR—search committee member and interviewer
PAUL—apostle of Christ

Set up long table in the middle of the stage with chairs around it to represent a boardroom. Place the chairs so that no one's back is to the audience. At the beginning, DYLAN, KAYLA, and CONNOR should be seated around the table, each with a pile of papers and a pen in front of them. They are all wearing business clothes. PAUL should be off stage, dressed in business casual—slightly more casual than the others but still looking nice.

DYLAN: That interview went well, don't you think?

[KAYLA and CONNOR nod and say "yes" or something similar and make notes on their papers in front of them.]

DYLAN: Kayla, please escort in our next candidate, Paul of Tarsus.

[KAYLA goes offstage and leads in PAUL in a welcoming manner.]

KAYLA: *[begins line while walking PAUL in]* Welcome, Paul. Thank you for taking time out of your busy schedule to interview with us. My name is Kayla, and this is Dylan and Connor.

[DYLAN and CONNOR stand up, and PAUL shakes each person's hand. Then all four sit down at the table.]

PAUL: Hello. Thank you. It's my pleasure to be here.

CONNOR: We, of course, are the ministry search committee of First Church. We have been interviewing several candidates for the position of student minister here. After the interviews we will make recommendations to the church leadership.

PAUL: I understand.

KAYLA: *[shuffles through her pile of papers and pulls one out]* We have your application here, and we'd like to ask you a few questions about what you have written. Could you clarify your responses for us?

PAUL: Yes, of course.

KAYLA: *[looks down as if reading from the paper]* In the section titled "Previous positions held," you listed "blasphemer, persecutor, violent man."

PAUL: That is correct.

DYLAN: You've got to be kidding!

PAUL: No. I'm quite serious.

CONNOR: You realize that those aren't exactly the kind of qualifications we're looking for.

PAUL: But they are the truth nonetheless. I regularly cursed Jesus' church, believing the Son of God was a phony and a liar.

DYLAN: And you were a persecutor?

PAUL: Indeed. I worked for the religious leaders in Jerusalem. They sent me to arrest men and women who claimed to be Christians. Then I threw them into prison.

KAYLA: And your history of violence?

PAUL: I could tell you many stories. One you might have heard of is my involvement in the illegal execution of a preacher named Stephen.

DYLAN: I must say that most candidates for this position tell very different stories about themselves!

KAYLA: It's true. We've seen some pretty impressive résumés.

PAUL: *[chuckling]* And you wonder why I describe myself as the worst of sinners.

DYLAN: It certainly doesn't sound like a good way to get a job.

PAUL: The fact is, what I have done shouldn't be labeled merely as youthful indiscretions or sowing wild oats. My actions were sinful. The evil I have done is real.

CONNOR: Pardon our amazement, Paul, but I'm sure we're all wondering why you are sitting in this room with us rather than in jail! Or at least hiding out someplace, afraid to show your face in polite society.

KAYLA: I would have to agree. Most people who have done the things you have done would be ashamed to admit it, let alone apply for a position of church leadership.

Paul: Then I believe they have missed the point.

Dylan: And what *is* the point?

Paul: That even the worst of sinners can start over.

Kayla: But surely you can't expect the members of our church to just forget your past?

Paul: We *do* serve a God who says that he no longer remembers our sins once we've been forgiven.

Connor: But certainly that doesn't mean *everything*!

Paul: Those who obey Christ Jesus have *no* condemnation. *No* means *no*, doesn't it?

Connor: Well . . .

Dylan: But why include your sordid past as . . . as credentials?

Kayla: Yes, why should someone like you ever be in a church leadership role?

Paul: Let me ask you some questions.

Connor: OK.

Paul: Would someone who was once overweight but is now fit and trim be a good person to lead a diet workshop?

Dylan: Uh . . . I guess so. Sure!

Paul: Would someone who was once poor but became rich by starting her own business be credible when teaching others how to make money?

Kayla: What does that have to do with anything?

Paul: As I have said before, I have been the worst of sinners. I was morally bankrupt before God. But now I am rich in his grace. Who better to lead others to believe in Jesus and receive eternal life?

Connor: I guess you *could* look at it that way . . .

Kayla: I'll need some time to think about that one.

Dylan: Paul, I believe you have answered all of our questions. We thank you again for speaking with us. We're going to continue our interviews and get back with you.

PAUL: I understand. I thank you for your time as well. *[gets up from the table, shakes each one's hand, and exits]*

DYLAN: Well, that was an interesting interview.

KAYLA: I'll say! Do you think we'll ever find someone to replace our student minister?

CONNOR: I don't know. It has taken us a while. We have to realize what a fine person used to lead this ministry. He might not be easily replaced.

DYLAN: True. Quality people like Judas Iscariot don't come along every day.

KAYLA: You know, when Judas left us, he went to join Jesus' inner circle. I wonder what ever happened to him? He sure was something!

>>> PURPOSE:

Use this parody of a makeover show to restate God's idea of beauty as described in Peter's first letter.

>>> PORTION OF SCRIPTURE:

1 Peter 3:1-8

>>> PROPS:

fashionable (but somewhat overdone) accessories that can easily be taken off during the skit: necklace, big earrings, hat, scarf, etc.
Bible

>>> PEOPLE:

HOST—female
SOPHIE COLDHART—attractive, soft-spoken young woman
JUSTIN COLDHART—strong but *not* obnoxious husband of Sophie
PETER—apostle of Jesus

SOPHIE and JUSTIN stand onstage, a good distance apart, with backs turned slightly to one another, and looking angry. SOPHIE is wearing all the fashion accessories. HOST stands in between them, center stage. Bible should be on the floor, unseen, near SOPHIE.

HOST: *[speaks to audience]* Tonight on *Absolute Alterations* . . . a couple struggles with difficulties in their marriage. We introduce you to Sophie Coldhart.

[HOST gestures toward SOPHIE.]

SOPHIE: My husband and I have been drifting apart for years. We seem to be heading in different directions . . . with different priorities.

HOST: And her husband, Justin Coldhart.

[HOST gestures toward JUSTIN.]

JUSTIN: She's not the woman I married. We used to have fun. Now all she wants to do is preach and nag.

HOST: Let's hear a little more of the story from each side. *[walks over to stand near SOPHIE and speaks to her]* Sophie?

SOPHIE: I've tried to make myself beautiful for Justin. I make sure my hair is always styled. I wear the latest fashions. I keep myself in shape. Justin never sees me without makeup and jewelry. But he never seems to notice. Or care . . .

HOST: I see. *[walks over to stand near JUSTIN and speaks to him]* And what's your side of the story, Justin?

JUSTIN: Sophie spends a fortune on herself. If she's not killing herself at the gym or getting her hair done, she's shopping for clothing or jewelry at the mall. I don't want a fashion model. I want the woman I married. I don't even know if she exists anymore . . .

[HOST walks back to center stage.]

HOST: *[to audience]* To help us with the Coldharts, *Absolute Alterations* turned to an expert in complete makeovers—Peter, son of John. Peter, come on out and join us.

[PETER enters and stands by HOST.]

HOST: Hi, Peter. Please explain for us your evaluation process.

[As PETER talks, PETER and HOST walk over to SOPHIE and stand on either side of her.]

PETER: Looking at the Coldharts, I decided I needed to start with Sophie. She had lost her focus. She was piling fashion accessories on the outside but neglecting her inner beauty. I helped Sophie realize that her husband desired internal, not external, beauty from her. We worked at giving her a classic look, an eternal beauty.

[PETER and HOST help SOPHIE remove her accessories: necklace, earrings, hat, scarf, etc., and place them on the floor.]

PETER: Then we were ready to take the next step. Though her activities with her church were important, Sophie stopped nagging her husband to join her. She quietly went on her own.

[PETER picks up the Bible and hands it to SOPHIE, who opens it and begins to read.]

PETER: Sophie was prayerfully determined to work on her own relationship with God, not her husband's relationship with God.

HOST: Wow! That's an interesting approach, Peter.

[As PETER says his next lines, he walks over to JUSTIN and guides him toward center stage, while HOST guides SOPHIE (still holding Bible) toward center stage as well so that JUSTIN and SOPHIE meet in the middle, with the HOST and PETER on either side of the two. JUSTIN looks at SOPHIE as if noticing what has changed about her, while she continues to hold the Bible open and smiles. They pantomime talking when PETER says his line about them having real conversation.]

PETER: With that pressure off, Sophie almost immediately began to notice a change in her relationship with Justin. He seemed to want to spend more time with her. And she found herself with less time for her weekly hair appointments and her shopping binges. They talked—real conversation, not just a list of demands fired back and forth, which had been typical of their marriage in recent years.

HOST: And Justin, you began to change when you noticed Sophie's change. Isn't that right?

JUSTIN: Very true. Sophie had begun going to a local church a few years ago. I was never interested. And the more she begged me to go, the more I resisted. I had become a Christian when I was a teen, but I stopped attending before Sophie and I met in college. But lately, the real change in her is sparking something in me. I've begun secretly looking at some of the Bible study books she has been reading. *[looks over SOPHIE's shoulder at her Bible]* The stories in the Bible of strong but gentle women like Sarah, the wife of Abraham, are fascinating. Lately Sophie seems to be acting more like those women rather than trying to be a fashion model.

SOPHIE: *[closes Bible and hugs it to her chest as she speaks]* To tell you the truth, the idea of being submissive to my husband scared me! I was sure he would take advantage of the situation. But just the opposite happened. Justin became so much more gentle than he had been in recent years. *[looks at JUSTIN and smiles]* I really feel respected and cherished.

PETER: So in this final step of this family makeover, both Sophie and Justin discovered beauty in relationships. Not only did their marriage blossom, they found themselves having deep and harmonious friendships with others.

[JUSTIN puts his arm around SOPHIE as they say their final lines.]

JUSTIN: Now we worship together. We have Christian friends. Our life is so different now than it was just six months ago.

SOPHIE: It's really hard to believe. We will always be grateful to Peter and the staff of *Absolute Alterations*. Thank you.

HOST: *[to audience]* What a beautiful story. Thanks to our makeover expert, Peter. And thanks to you for watching *Absolute Alterations*.